D0438025

LITTLE WORLD
A Book About Tolerance

Banana Patch Press

Library of Congress Control Number: 2001119354
ISBN 0-9715333-5-0

Printed in the United States of America

LITTLE WORLD

A Book About Tolerance

By

Joanna F. Carolan

Acknowledgements

Special thanks to:

My husband, Dr. Terry Carolan, and my mother, Nancy Forbes, for their continuous support, encouragement, and for reading my many drafts

Tom Niblick, at Barefoot Design Studio on Kaua'i, for his book design, expertise, and his patience

Donn Forbes, Jana Viles, Sheri Boulay, Gayla McCarthy, Sara and Juan David Velez, Elizabeth Carolan, and Lisa Forbes, for their helpful comments and suggestions

Kathy Graham for her web-site design

Carol Bain, of Kaua'i WorldWide Communications, for her marketing assistance

The Banana Patch crew: Rhye Daub, Duane Krewson, Chase Collins, Megan O'Connell, Nate Cushman, and support team: Janice Lum, and Jeff Soulier

Jenet Miller, Sahna Carmona, Ken "Milo" Milosky, Mayor Maryanne Kusaka, Steve Busch, Scott and Laura Phillipson, Jack Pomeroy, Renee Fujii, Dianna Soong, Christine and Larry Reisor, Debbie Costello, Linda and Jimmy Wray, Tom Munson, Ron Shoji, Diana Taylor, Herb and Cindy Schoenhardt, who have supported my work as an artist

Michael and Diane Sears, Karl Forbes, Stephan Sears, Ripley Sears, Andrew Sears, Nonae Sears, my Sears cousins, Karin Burmeister, Pauline White, William O'Brien, Doron Weinberg, Jenny Moalem, Dennis Ikel, Linda Aiello, and David Servi, who have helped "shape" my world.

Thank you all from the bottom of my heart.

For
My mother,
"Teacher Nancy"

There was a little world
Spinning in a great big sky,
With lands, oceans, rivers,
Lakes, and mountains high.

On one side of this world
Was a square little land

Where square flowers grew
In square bits of sand.

In this square land
Lived square little people.
They built square churches,
Each had a square steeple.

They lived in square houses
With square little doors.
They rowed in square boats
With square little oars.

They walked their square dogs
On little square streets.
They hugged their square children.
They ate square sweets.

They prayed to a square God;
They felt they were blessed.
Squares were all they had,
So they thought squares were best.

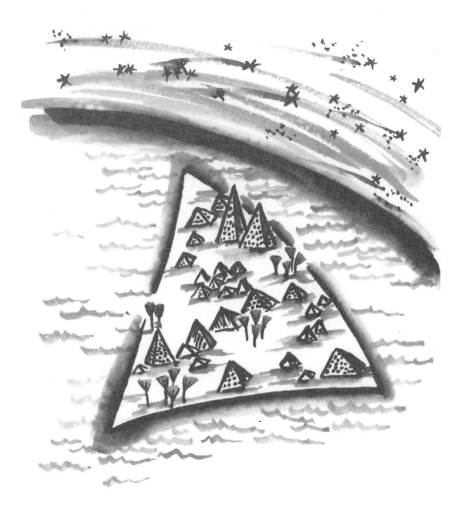

In another place on this world
Was land shaped like a triangle.

Triangular plants grew there,
Flowers and leaves, all in a tangle.

The little people of this land
Were triangular, too.
They kept triangular animals
In a little triangular zoo.

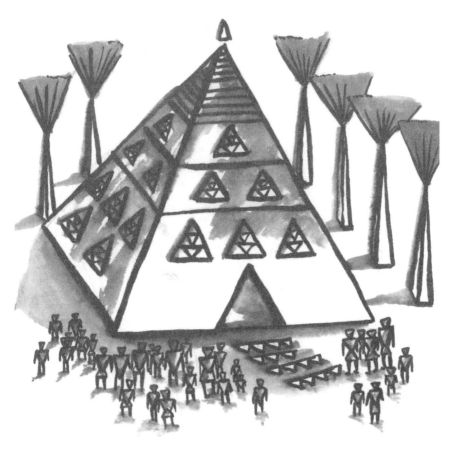

They built triangular temples,
And wore triangular shoes.
Their little triangular windows
Looked out on triangular views.

They rode triangular bicycles

Down little triangular lanes.

They hugged their triangular children.

They washed triangular window panes.

They knew no other land;
Triangles were all they saw.
They praised triangular Gods,
And believed triangles were law.

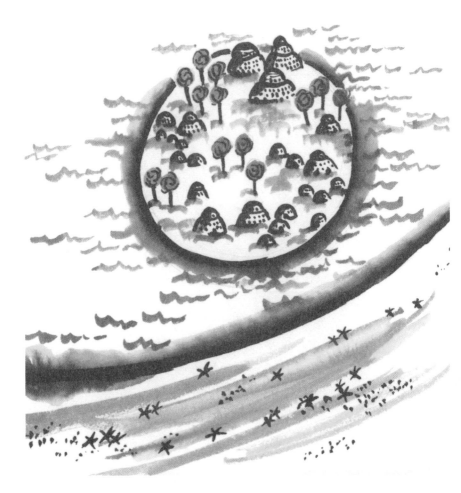

In another part of this world

Was a country completely round.

Round leaves grew on round trees;

Round grass covered the ground.

The little people there were round,
And they wore round hats.
They prayed in round mosques,
And they sat on round mats.

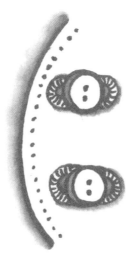

Their clothes had round buttons
That fit into round holes.
They ate round noodles
From little round bowls.

They sailed in round boats

On little round lakes.

They hugged their round children.

They ate little round cakes.

Their God was round,

Round was all they knew.

Although they hadn't seen them,

Wouldn't other lands be round, too?

And in a further corner of this world

Was a little rectangular spot.

Rectangular people lived there

And the weather was very hot.

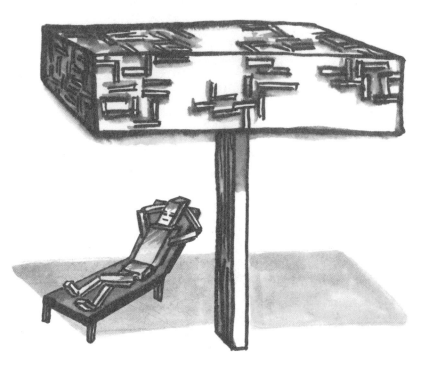

These little rectangular people

Lived in rectangular homes,

And they styled their rectangular hair

With little rectangular combs.

They visited rectangular shrines.

They drove rectangular trucks.

They hugged their rectangular children.

They raised little rectangular ducks.

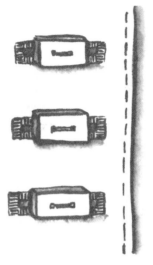

Their clothes had rectangular buttons
That fit into rectangular holes.
They flew rectangular flags
From little rectangular poles.

They worshiped rectangular Gods,
And sang their praises on high.
The rectangle was all they knew;
They didn't ask why.

Then … on one particular day,

People gathered on every shore.

Groups from every country

Decided to explore.

Each place sent out boats

To search across the sea.

Round, triangle, square, rectangle,

What a surprise it would be!

They traveled for weeks

Across oceans vast and wide.

All the time wondering

What was on the other side.

As the first little boats

Reached a distant shore,

Can you imagine the confusion,

Astonishment, and more?

As square little people

Discovered round trees,

And triangular people
Saw their first rectangular bees,

As rectangular eyes looked
At triangular faces,
And round people saw
Rectangular places,

As round eyes stared at

Rectangular pea pods,

And square ears heard of

Triangular Gods,

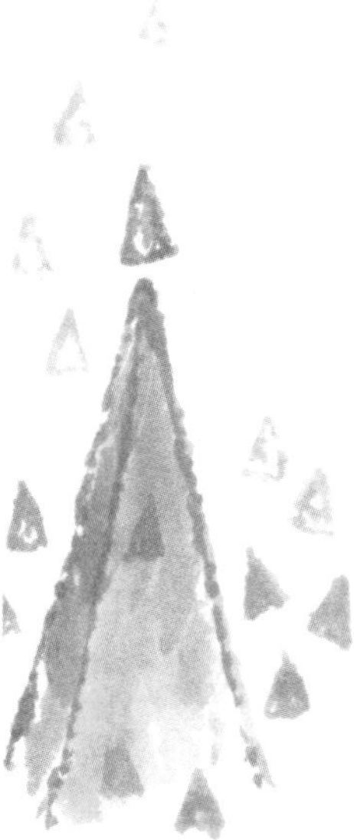

Some people were shocked.

Some felt sad.

Some were afraid.

Some got mad.

They saw so many differences,

They said, it's too strange.

They didn't understand;

They said, you must change!

This is not what we wanted

When we traveled so long.

You should be like us.

Your ways are all wrong!

Triangular shoes can't fit
Rectangular feet.
A round wrapper can't wrap
A square sweet.

A square person can't sit on

A triangular chair.

A rectangular comb can't style

A round person's hair.

How can round cars

Drive on square lanes?

How can round windows

Use square window panes?

How can a triangular hat

Fit a rectangular head?

How can triangular sheets

Fit a rectangular bed?

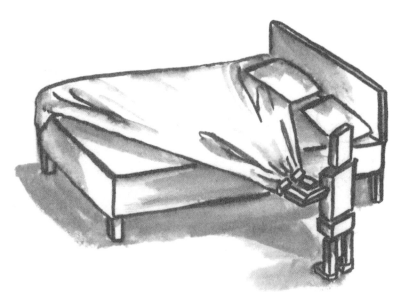

Can a round button

Fit a rectangular hole?

Can we eat triangular pie

From a square bowl?

Can we still hug our children?

Can we still wear our hats?

Can we still walk our dogs?

Can we still pet our cats?

Can we accept our differences,

But see how we are alike?

Can we put round wheels

On a triangular bike?

Can we worship different Gods

With many different voices?

Can we live together peacefully

And have more choices?

Who knows which is better,

A round or square song?

What shape is a heart?

Is any shape wrong?

Some shapes work better
Together than alone.
A triangle and a circle
Make an ice cream cone!

In fact … round buttons fit fine
In rectangular holes.

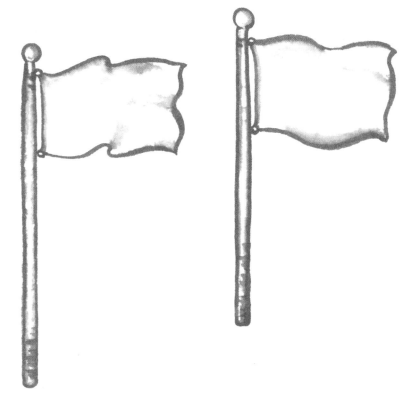

And ... rectangular flags fly well

From round flag poles.

Triangular wings work great

On a round bodied plane.

Rectangular tracks fit perfectly

The round wheels of a train.

Gifts are always welcome
In any shape or size.
And any shape is good
For cakes and pies!

If we combine all our shapes
What can we do?
If we all work together
Can we build something new?

We can build a kinder world
With respect and caring.
We can build a better world
By giving and sharing.

We can build a playful world
In which we all have fun.
We can build a plentiful world
With enough for everyone.

We can build a safer world

One that is peaceful and free.

We can build a tolerant world

And … it starts with you and me.

The Beginning.

ORDER FORM

Order direct from Banana Patch Press:

By Mail: Banana Patch Press
             P.O. Box 840
             Lawai, HI 96765
By Fax: (808) 332-7311
By Phone: (808) 332-5944
             (800) 914-5944 toll-free
On line: www.bananapatchpress.com

Please send the following:

Quantity:	Title:	Price:	Total:
____	LITTLE WORLD, A Book About Tolerance	$14.95ea	____

Shipping:			
	One (1) book	$5.00	____
	Each add'l. book	$2.00	____

Grand Total: ____

Mailing Address:

Name: _____

Address: _____

City: _____ State: _____ Zip: _____

Telephone: (_____) _____

Method of Payment:

❑ Check

❑ Credit Card: ❑ Visa   ❑ MasterCard   ❑ Discover

Card Number: _____

Name on Card: _____ Exp. Date: _____ / _____

Call (800) 914-5944 *toll free*
and order now